## CAMBRIDGE
UNIVERSITY PRESS

## CAMBRIDGE ENGLISH
### Language Assessment
Part of the University of Cambridge

CAMBRIDGE
OFFICIAL
PREPARATION MATERIAL

Cambridge English

# Movers

AUTHENTIC
EXAMINATION
PAPERS **2**

T0349639

## STUDENT'S BOOK

**Cambridge University Press**
www.cambridge.org/elt

**Cambridge English Language Assessment**
www.cambridgeenglish.org

Information on this title: www.cambridge.org/9781316636244

© Cambridge University Press and UCLES 2018

This publication is in copyright. Subject to statutory exception
and to the provisions of relevant collective licensing agreements,
no reproduction of any part may take place without the written
permission of Cambridge University Press.

First published 2018

20  19  18  17  16  15  14  13  12  11  10  9

Printed in Malaysia by Vivar Printing

*A catalogue record for this publication is available from the British Library*

ISBN 978-1-316-63624-4 Student's Book
ISBN 978-1-316-63627-5 Answer Booklet
ISBN 978-1-316-63630-5 Audio CDs (2)

The publishers have no responsibility for the persistence or accuracy of URLs
for external or third-party internet websites referred to in this publication, and
do not guarantee that any content on such websites is, or will remain, accurate
or appropriate. Information regarding prices, travel timetables, and other factual
information given in this work is correct at the time of first printing but the
publishers do not guarantee the accuracy of such information thereafter.

Cover Illustration: (whale) Ilyaf/iStock/Getty Images Plus; (surfboard) filo/iStock/Getty Images Plus;
(books) adekvat/iStock/Getty Images Plus

# <u>Contents</u>

## Test 1

Listening                                    4

Reading and Writing                         12

## Test 2

Listening                                   26

Reading and Writing                         34

## Test 3

Listening                                   48

Reading and Writing                         56

## Speaking Tests

Test 1                                      70

Test 2                                      74

Test 3                                      78

## Listening

# Part 1

**– 5 questions –**

**Listen and draw lines. There is one example.**

Fred                    Jack                    Clare                    Zoe

Peter                              Paul                              Julia

# Part 2

**– 5 questions –**

**Listen and write. There is one example.**

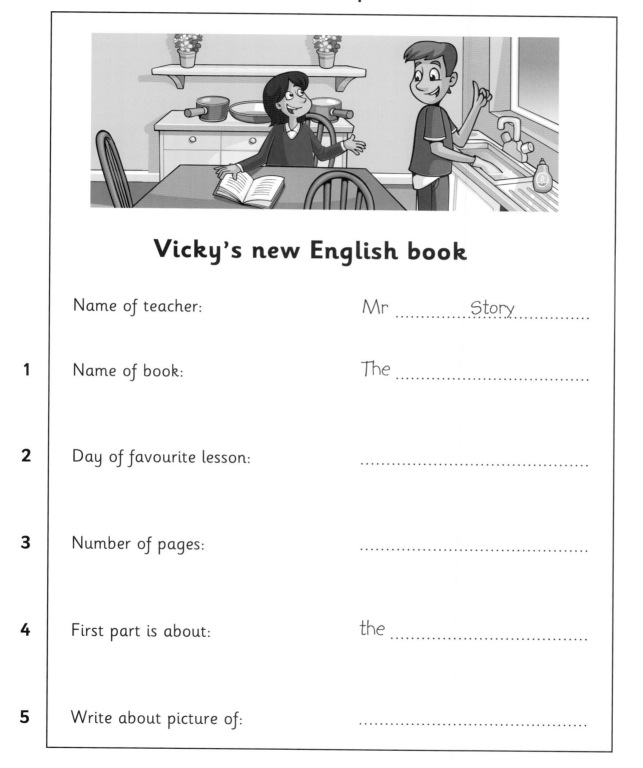

### Vicky's new English book

|   |   |   |
|---|---|---|
|   | Name of teacher: | Mr .......... Story .......... |
| 1 | Name of book: | The .......... |
| 2 | Day of favourite lesson: | .......... |
| 3 | Number of pages: | .......... |
| 4 | First part is about: | the .......... |
| 5 | Write about picture of: | .......... |

# Part 3

### – 5 questions –

**What does Jim's grandpa enjoy doing in these places?**

**Listen and write a letter in each box. There is one example.**

library    E

park    ☐

station    ☐

sports centre    ☐

cinema    ☐

shopping centre    ☐

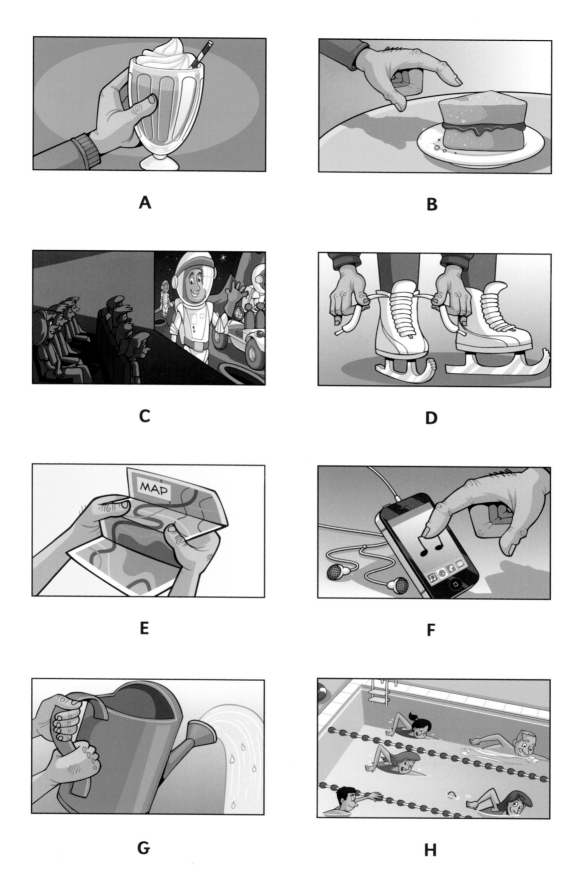

A

B

C

D

E

F

G

H

# Part 4

**– 5 questions –**

**Listen and tick (✔) the box. There is one example.**

What can Daisy do now?

A ✔          B ☐          C ☐

**1**  Where is Lily?

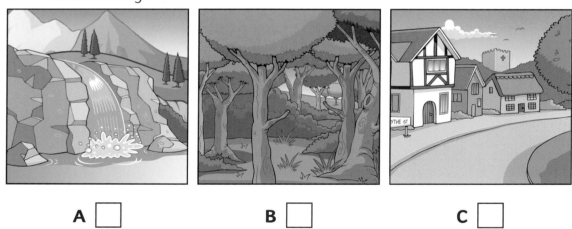

A ☐          B ☐          C ☐

**2**  Which is Charlie's dad?

A ☐          B ☐          C ☐

**3** What did Sally see?

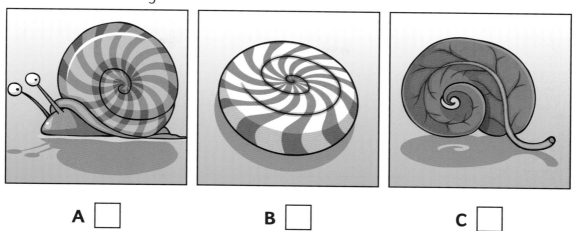

A ☐        B ☐        C ☐

**4** Who does Nick want to phone?

A ☐        B ☐        C ☐

**5** What is the matter with Eva?

A ☐        B ☐        C ☐

# Part 5

### – 5 questions –

**Listen and colour and write. There is one example.**

Choose a

Blank Page

## Reading and Writing

# Part 1
### – 5 questions –

Look and read. Choose the correct words and write them on the lines. There is one example.

a clown

mountains

a forest

a doctor

cheese

a picnic

a film star

tea

## Example

This is often yellow and many people eat it
between some bread.                                  ............cheese............

## Questions

**1**   When you go to a cinema you can
see this person.                                    ...................................

**2**   Some people like climbing these and
you can often see snow on the top.                  ...................................

**3**   This is food that you take to eat outside.   ...................................

**4**   This person works in a hospital
with people who are sick.                           ...................................

**5**   There are always lots of trees
in this place.                                      ...................................

# Part 2

## – 6 questions –

**Read the text and choose the best answer.**

**Example**

| Jim: | Hi, Vicky! Is that your new comic? |
|---|---|

Vicky:
    A   It's OK.
    B   Yes, it is.
    C   It is mine.

**Questions**

**1**   **Jim:**              What are you reading about?

    **Vicky:**
    A   I'm good at drawing.
    B   What's the matter?
    C   An old pirate ship.

**2**   **Jim:**          Which is the best part of your comic?

    **Vicky:**          A   This page. Look!
                B   Come on! Here.
                C   Let's go! Quick!

**3**   **Jim:**          Which day do you get your comic?

    **Vicky:**          A   In the afternoon.
                B   Every Wednesday.
                C   Not this week.

**4**   **Jim:**          Does your dad buy your comic for you?

    **Vicky:**          A   Yes. So do I, Jim.
                B   They're my mother's.
                C   I ask my uncle to get it.

**5**   **Jim:**          I really like comics.

    **Vicky:**          A   Well, you can read this, too.
                B   Because I'm on this page.
                C   I'm sorry. I don't know.

**6**   **Jim:**          Can you give me your comic now?

    **Vicky:**          A   Me too! Goodbye!
                B   All right! Here you are.
                C   No thank you, Jim!

# Part 3

### – 6 questions –

**Read the story. Choose a word from the box. Write the correct word next to numbers 1–5. There is one example.**

Julia's family had a pet donkey. He was called Dan. The family didn't

........................ *ride* ........................ Dan. The donkey had fun in their field and

ate the **(1)** ........................................ that grew there and the vegetables

and fruit that Julia gave him every morning. 'Hi, Dan! Look! Carrots

and apples for you today!' Julia said last Friday. But the donkey

didn't **(2)** ........................................ to her. 'Don't you want any food,

Dan? Are you ill?' Julia asked and went back to the house to tell her

**(3)** ........................................ . 'Don't worry!' Julia's father said. 'Oh listen.

That's my phone.' When he came back he said, 'Now we understand.

Dan isn't **(4)** ........................................ because he ate all the pears on Mrs

Cook's tree last night! Naughty donkey!' 'But we love him,' Mum said. 'We

must go and say sorry to Mrs Cook. Let's take her a carrot cake and an

apple **(5)** ........................................ . She likes those!' 'Dan does too!'

Julia laughed.

## Example

ride

angry

pie

grass

farm

hungry

run

shout

parents

**(6)  Now choose the best name for the story.**

**Tick one box.**

Dan and the pear tree ☐

Mrs Cook's pet donkey ☐

Julia's very good idea ☐

# Part 4
### – 5 questions –

**Read the text. Choose the right words and write them on the lines.**

## Blue whales

**Example**   Some blue whales are longer ............*than*............ three buses!

They are the largest animals in the world. They eat the very smallest

**1**   animals that live in the sea and .............................. fish

eggs, too.

**2**   Blue whales live in cold seas most .............................. the

year because they can find more food there. But when there is ice on

**3**   the water, .............................. whales swim to another part of

**4**   the world. There, they .............................. . When there is no ice,

they swim back again! Blue whales don't have teeth. They have a kind of

**5**   moustache inside .............................. mouths which catches the

food when they swim.

| **Example** | than | after | into |
|---|---|---|---|
| **1** | first | here | sometimes |
| **2** | with | of | at |
| **3** | these | both | lots |
| **4** | wait | waited | waiting |
| **5** | theirs | them | their |

# Part 5
### – 7 questions –

**Look at the pictures and read the story. Write some words to
complete the sentences about the story. You can use 1, 2 or 3 words.**

### <u>Snow day</u>

It snowed every year in Charlie's village.

The weather was worse this year. Charlie's school had to close and his
parents couldn't go shopping or go to work. It was too dangerous to drive
their small car.

## Examples

The people in .......*Charlie's village*....... saw snow on the ground every year.

In the bad weather this year, Charlie couldn't go to ...........*school*........... .

## Questions

**1**  Charlie's parents couldn't go to work or do any .................................. .

**2**  It wasn't safe to travel in the family's .................................. .

I'd like to make some pancakes but we haven't got any milk or eggs!' Mum said on Monday morning.

'We need toothpaste, too,' Dad said.

'That's OK,' said Charlie. 'We can get things like that on the internet! I know a good website!'

'Why doesn't it stop snowing?' said Mum that afternoon. 'Oh, I'd like to be on holiday and see the sun! And I wanted to go and get tickets for the circus today!'

'That's OK,' said Charlie. 'I can show you pictures of sunny holiday places on the internet and a website where you can buy circus tickets!'

**3** On Monday morning, Charlie's mother needed ................................... and his dad needed toothpaste.

**4** Charlie knew a ................................... where people could buy things for the home.

**5** Charlie found some photos of ................................... for his mother to look at on the internet.

So the family sat around the computer and bought the things they needed and looked at photos.

Then Charlie said, 'Now I've got to do my homework. Can you help me, Dad? I've got to write about the moon.'

'Sorry, Charlie,' Dad said. 'I can't help . . . but look! Here's a good website!'

**6**  For his ..................................... , Charlie had to write about the moon.

**7**  Charlie's father couldn't ..................................... Charlie, but he showed him a good website!

Blank Page

# Part 6

**– 6 questions –**

**Look and read and write.**

**Examples**

Opposite the bus station, there is a ................... *park* ................... .

What can you see in the sky?   *a helicopter and some clouds*

## Questions

**Complete the sentences.**

**1**   The young boy is ..................................... .

**2**   You can see a map next to the ..................................... .

**Answer the questions.**

**3**   What is the little girl wearing?

..................................................................................

**4**   What can people buy from the café?

..................................................................................

**Now write two sentences about the picture.**

**5**   ..................................................................................

**6**   ..................................................................................

## Listening

# Part 1
– 5 questions –

**Listen and draw lines. There is one example.**

Zoe                Paul                Clare                Jim

Charlie                Daisy                Julia

# Part 2
### – 5 questions –

**Listen and write. There is one example.**

## Sally's trip to the funfair

|   | | |
|---|---|---|
| | When: | .........Saturday......... afternoon |
| **1** | Favourite ride: | ........................................... |
| **2** | Animals in the field: | ........................................... |
| **3** | Name of game: | ............................... the fish |
| **4** | Food: | ........................................... |
| **5** | She saw friend: | ........................................... |

# Part 3

### – 5 questions –

**What did Jack and Jane do in these places?**

**Listen and write a letter in each box. There is one example.**

market [C]

circus ☐

farm ☐

swimming pool ☐

forest ☐

city centre ☐

# Part 4
### – 5 questions –

**Listen and tick (✔) the box. There is one example.**

What is Vicky's brother's work?

A ☐ B ✔ C ☐

**1** What does Fred want to eat?

A ☐ B ☐ C ☐

**2** Where is the cat?

A ☐ B ☐ C ☐

**3**    What is Lily doing now?

**A** ☐        **B** ☐        **C** ☐

**4**    What did Peter do today?

**A** ☐        **B** ☐        **C** ☐

**5**    What is the weather like today?

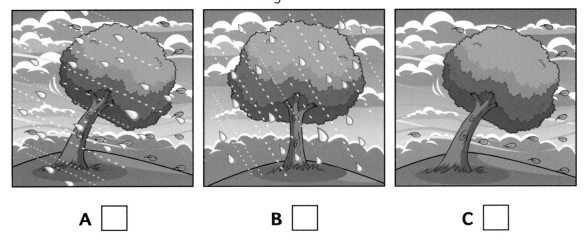

**A** ☐        **B** ☐        **C** ☐

# Part 5

## – 5 questions –

Listen and colour and write. There is one example.

Blank Page

# Reading and Writing

## Part 1

### – 5 questions –

Look and read. Choose the correct words and write them on the lines. There is one example.

a farmer

a kangaroo

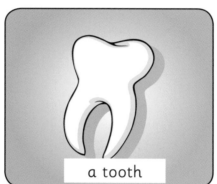

a tooth

a doctor

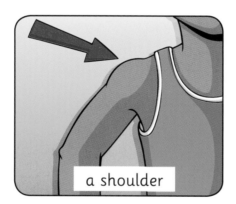

a shoulder

a pirate

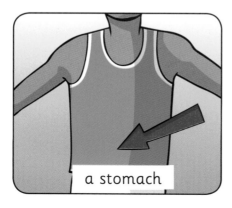

a stomach

a panda

## Example

This person sometimes works in the fields.  ............ *a farmer* ............

## Questions

**1**  This part of your body is at
the top of your arm.                    ...................................

**2**  In stories, this person sails around the
world in a big ship.                    ...................................

**3**  This person works with nurses
in a hospital.                          ...................................

**4**  You can find this in your mouth.
It's white.                             ...................................

**5**  This animal moves quickly.
It can jump very well.                  ...................................

# Part 2
### – 6 questions –

**Read the text and choose the best answer.**

**Example**

**Charlie:**        What did you do last night, Daisy?

**Daisy:**
- (A)  I watched a film.
- B  I don't watch films.
- C  I love watching films.

**Questions**

**1**  **Charlie:**        Last week, I watched a film about aliens. Did you see it, too?

**Daisy:**
- A  Yes, so do I!
- B  Yes, it was really great!
- C  Yes, it's tonight.

**2  Charlie:**     Which alien did you like best in the film?

   **Daisy:**        A   One of the aliens.
                     B   He was my favourite one.
                     C   The one with the orange eyes.

**3  Charlie:**     Do you like watching funny films?

   **Daisy:**        A   Me too.
                     B   They're OK.
                     C   You're all right.

**4  Charlie:**     How about coming to my house to watch
                    *Happy Families* on TV?

   **Daisy:**        A   Would you like to?
                     B   I think you're well.
                     C   That's a good idea.

**5  Charlie:**     Ben Brown's in the film. Do you know him?

   **Daisy:**        A   Yes, he's got a beard.
                     B   Yes, he's called Ben.
                     C   No, he doesn't.

**6  Charlie:**     Shall I get some drinks for us?

   **Daisy:**        A   OK, and I can buy chocolate.
                     B   OK, it's here.
                     C   OK, I can help him.

# Part 3

**– 6 questions –**

**Read the story. Choose a word from the box. Write the correct word next to numbers 1–5. There is one example.**

It was Vicky's birthday last Saturday. Her aunt took her to the town centre. She wanted to ................*buy*................ Vicky a new sweater for her birthday. They went to Vicky's favourite

**(1)** ...................................... . Vicky wanted a blue sweater but all the blue ones were too small.

'Oh dear,' said her aunt. 'What about the red one?'

'It's nice,' said Vicky. 'But I don't need another red sweater.' They couldn't find a sweater that Vicky liked.

Vicky was tired and **(2)** ...................................... . 'Let's go to the new café. You can have a **(3)** ...................................... of lemonade and we can both have some cake,' her aunt said.

Vicky had some chocolate cake and a drink. Vicky enjoyed her chocolate cake and drink but she didn't want to do any more shopping.

When they got home, Vicky's grandma was there.

'Happy Birthday, Vicky,' she said and gave her a

**(4)** ...................................... to open. It was a beautiful blue sweater.

Vicky **(5)** ...................................... , 'Thank you, Grandma. That's the sweater I really wanted!'

## Example

| | | |
|---|---|---|
| buy | laughed | thirsty |
| blanket | glass | strong |
| present | carried | shop |

**(6)   Now choose the best name for the story.**

**Tick one box.**

An exciting place ☐

Mum's new clothes ☐

Vicky's shopping trip ☐

# Part 4

### – 5 questions –

**Read the text. Choose the right words and write them on the lines.**

## Rabbits

**Example**  When you go for a walk .................. in .................. the forest or

countryside and move quietly, you sometimes see a rabbit!

**1**  ................................. funny little animals have long ears and

brown, grey or white bodies. They have strong legs

**2**  ................................. they can't run. They hop, like kangaroos,

from one place to another.

**3**  When they are hopping, ................................. is easy to see their

small white round tails.

Rabbits sleep under the ground and only come up

**4**  ................................. play or find food. They don't eat meat.

They eat grass and vegetables.

**5**  Some families have a pet rabbit that ................................. in their

garden. Does yours?

| Example | in | at | on |
|---|---|---|---|
| 1 | This | Every | These |
| 2 | but | because | then |
| 3 | there | it | some |
| 4 | for | to | with |
| 5 | live | living | lives |

# Part 5

### – 7 questions –

**Look at the pictures and read the story. Write some words to complete the sentences about the story. You can use 1, 2 or 3 words.**

## The picnic

Clare and Peter lived in a small flat. On Sundays, the family always went to the park to play different games, because they didn't have a garden.

Last Sunday morning, Mum said, 'Let's take a picnic too, today!' She made eight cheese sandwiches and Dad went shopping. He bought some grapes, salad leaves and four small fruit pies from the supermarket.

They drove to the park at one o'clock.

## Examples

Clare and Peter's family went to the park every .............. *Sunday* ..............

Last Sunday, Mum made ....... *eight sandwiches* ....... to put in the picnic.

## Questions

**1**  Dad bought some drinks and more food from

.................................. .

**2**  It was .................................. when the family got in their car to go to the park.

They played badminton and then sat down on some grass next to the lake. The family always enjoyed eating outside and everyone was hungry. They ate seven of the sandwiches and all four fruit pies first.

**3**   After their game of ..................................... , they sat down on some grass.

**4**   The family had some sandwiches and the ..................................... first.

Then some pretty little birds flew down to their picnic rug.

'They're hungry too,' said Clare and gave them three grapes and some salad leaves but the birds didn't eat them.

Then one of the birds flew on to Mum's shoulder. She looked at it and said, 'Oh, OK!' and gave the birds the last cheese sandwich! They loved it!

'How did you know that?' Clare asked. Mum smiled but didn't say anything. 'Mothers understand all kinds of things!' Dad said. 'You are brilliant, Mum!' Peter and Clare said.

**5** The birds didn't want any grapes or ................................. .

**6** ................................. gave the last sandwich to the birds.

**7** Peter and Clare think their mother is .................................!

Blank Page

# Part 6
## – 6 questions –

**Look and read and write.**

**Examples**

The baby is playing with a .................. clown .................. .

What's on the table next to the book?    .................. a small radio ..................

## Questions

**Complete the sentences.**

1    The boys are having a game of ..................................... .

2    The dog is sitting on the ground near the ..................................... .

**Answer the questions.**

3    Where is the cat?

.............................................................................................

4    What's the girl in the black skirt doing?

.............................................................................................

**Now write two sentences about the picture.**

5    .............................................................................................

6    .............................................................................................

# Part 1
**– 5 questions –**

**Listen and draw lines. There is one example.**

Vicky          Sam          Peter          Daisy

Pat                          Lily                          Paul

# Part 2
## – 5 questions –

**Listen and write. There is one example.**

## Uncle Charlie's new apartment

Where:             opposite ............. the river .........

**1**    Number of floors in building:     ...............................................

**2**    Favourite part of apartment:     ...............................................

**3**    Can have pets that are:     quiet and ...............................

**4**    Day to see Uncle Charlie:     ...............................................

**5**    Get off bus at:     ............................... Street

# Part 3

**– 5 questions –**

**Where must Jack put these things?**

**Listen and write a letter in each box. There is one example.**

| | | |
|---|---|---|
| | rulers | F |
| | a guitar | ☐ |
| | a photo | ☐ |
| | a rubber | ☐ |
| | homework | ☐ |
| | a jacket | ☐ |

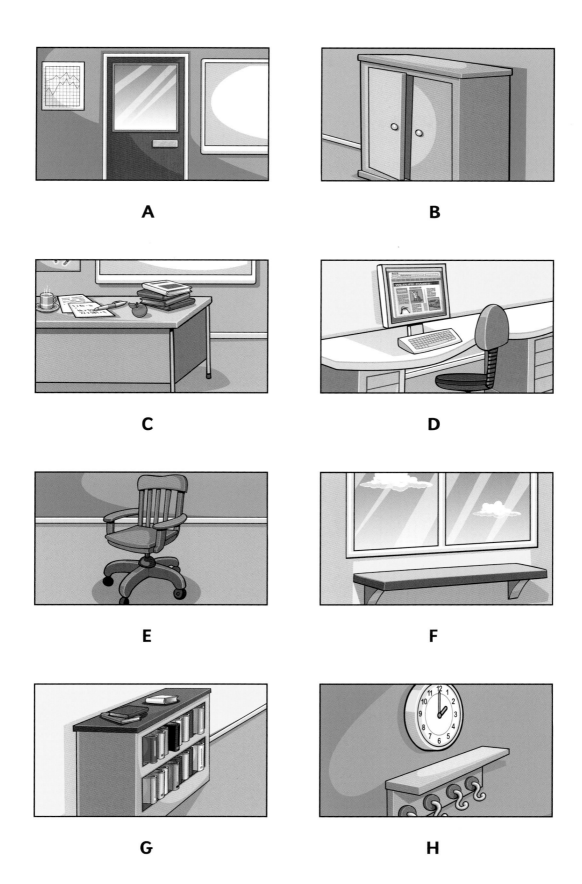

A

B

C

D

E

F

G

H

# Part 4
### – 5 questions –

**Listen and tick (✔) the box. There is one example.**

What did Anna do at the farm?

A ✔  B ☐  C ☐

**1**   Who is on Grace's poster?

A ☐  B ☐  C ☐

**2**   What can Aunt Lucy have in her tea?

  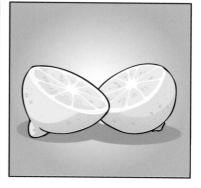

A ☐  B ☐  C ☐

**3** What is Sally doing now?

A ☐          B ☐          C ☐

**4** What must Fred take to the picnic?

A ☐          B ☐          C ☐

**5** Which is Clare's favourite day of the week?

A ☐          B ☐          C ☐

# Part 5

## – 5 questions –

Listen and colour and write. There is one example.

Blank Page

# Part 1
*– 5 questions –*

Look and read. Choose the correct words and write them on the lines. There is one example.

a cup

a supermarket

a lake

a mountain

a library

a star

a cinema

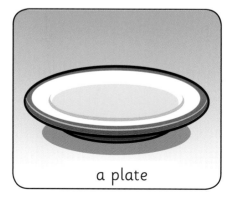

a plate

## Example

People go to this place to watch films.          .................. a cinema ..................

## Questions

**1**   You can go to this place to fish
or to sail a boat.                               ....................................

**2**   People put pancakes and other
food on this.                                    ....................................

**3**   People can read books here or
take them home.                                  ....................................

**4**   You drink your tea or coffee from this.  ....................................

**5**   You can see this at night when
it's not cloudy.                                 ....................................

# Part 2
### – 6 questions –

**Read the text and choose the best answer.**

**Example**

| | |
|---|---|
| **Paul:** | What did you do at the weekend, Jack? |
| **Jack:** | Ⓐ I went to the new sports centre.<br>B I like the new sports centre.<br>C I'm at the new sports centre. |

**Questions**

| | | |
|---|---|---|
| **1** | **Paul:** | Where is the new sports centre? |
| | **Jack:** | A It's very big.<br>B We saw it on the map.<br>C It's opposite the station. |

**2** **Paul:**     Did your parents take you to the
sports centre?

**Jack:**     A   No, I went with my uncle.
B   No, I think my cousin is there.
C   No, she was going to see my aunt.

**3** **Paul:**     Is there a swimming pool at the
sports centre?

**Jack:**     A   All right, that's fantastic.
B   When do you go there?
C   Yes, it's a really nice one.

**4** **Paul:**     I love doing sport.

**Jack:**     A   That's right.
B   Me too.
C   Come on.

**5** **Paul:**     Let's go to that sports centre this afternoon!

**Jack:**     A   Good idea!
B   I'm better!
C   Well done!

**6** **Paul:**     Shall I ask my mum to drive us to the
sports centre?

**Jack:**     A   Yes, I am.
B   Is she?
C   OK, thanks.

# Part 3

### – 6 questions –

**Read the story. Choose a word from the box. Write the correct word next to numbers 1–5. There is one example.**

Lily's class are learning about animals. Yesterday they walked to a

.................._farm_.................. near their school. Lily wore her new scarf because

it was a **(1)** ................................. day. She walked with her friend

Jane, and they talked about their favourite animals. 'I like horses,' said Lily.

'Oh, I don't!' said Jane. 'I'm **(2)** ................................. of them. I

like rabbits.'

The farmer showed the children his animals. The cows were in a big

**(3)** ................................. outside and the sheep, goats and chickens

were inside. 'Do you have any questions?' said the farmer.

'Yes,' said Jane. 'What do you feed your goats?'

'Different **(4)** ................................. ,' said the farmer.

'Well, why is that goat eating a scarf?' asked Jane.

'Oh no!' shouted Lily. 'That's mine!'

The farmer quickly took the scarf from the goat. 'I think my goats are really

**(5)** ................................. today!' he laughed. 'Would you like to give

them something to eat?'

## Example

| | | |
|---|---|---|
| farm | hungry | road |
| sunny | cold | field |
| afraid | picnic | vegetables |

**(6)   Now choose the best name for the story.**

**Tick one box.**

A naughty animal ☐

Lily's new pet ☐

A ride on a horse ☐

# Part 4

### – 5 questions –

**Read the text. Choose the right words and write them on the lines.**

## The jungle

**Example**  A jungle is a kind .............................of............................. forest. In jungles

**1**  the weather is hot and it often rains. The .......................................

jungle in the world is called the Amazon.

The leaves of plants are very big in these hot and wet places. It is really

**2**  difficult for people to walk in the jungle .......................................

they often can't see the ground!

Tigers, snakes, monkeys and parrots are some of the animals

**3**  ..................................... live in the jungle.

**4**  ..................................... jungle animals live above the ground.

**5**  In some jungles, there are frogs that can .......................................

between the trees!

| **Example** | for | of | from |
|---|---|---|---|
| **1** | largest | larger | large |
| **2** | because | than | or |
| **3** | who | which | what |
| **4** | Another | Every | Many |
| **5** | flew | flying | fly |

# Part 5

### – 7 questions –

**Look at the pictures and read the story. Write some words to complete the sentences about the story. You can use 1, 2 or 3 words.**

### <u>Charlie's birthday</u>

It was Charlie's birthday last Tuesday. When he woke up he was very excited. He got dressed quickly and went downstairs. 'Happy Birthday!' his brother shouted and he gave Charlie a brilliant new computer game. Then Charlie went into the kitchen and saw a very big present. It was from his parents. 'Wow!' said Charlie. 'Can I open it now?'

'Yes,' said Mum.

It was a bike. 'Thank you!' he said. 'It's the bike which I wanted the most.'

For breakfast his mum made Charlie his favourite chocolate pancakes.

## Examples

On Tuesday Charlie was .......<u>very excited</u>....... because it was his birthday.

Charlie got a computer game from .........<u>his brother</u>......... .

## Questions

**1**  There was a ........................... in the kitchen, and Charlie opened it.

**2**  Charlie got the ................................... that he really wanted.

**3**  Charlie ate ................................... for breakfast.

After breakfast Charlie's mum said, 'Come on, Charlie, we have to go shopping now.'

'But it's my birthday! I want to do fun things on my birthday! Shopping's boring!' Charlie said. 'I want to invite my best friend to play my new computer game.' 'Sorry, Charlie, we have to go now,' his mum said.

**4** Charlie didn't want to ..................................... on his birthday.

**5** Charlie wanted his ..................................... to come to his house.

When they got home later, Charlie's mum said, 'You go inside first, Charlie.' When Charlie opened the door, he saw all his friends and family. They shouted, 'Happy Birthday, Charlie!' Charlie was very surprised.

They played some games and then they ate lots of party food and some birthday cake.

Charlie's birthday wasn't boring, it was fantastic! 'Thanks, Mum,' Charlie said. 'I really enjoyed the party.'

**6**   When he got home, Charlie was ..................................... because all his friends and family were in his house.

**7**   Charlie loved his party and had a ..................................... birthday.

**Picture Story**

Clare's birthday

Clare

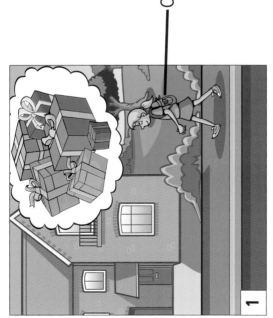

**Odd-one-out**

Blank Page

Find the Differences

**Picture Story**

Fred and the tiger

Fred

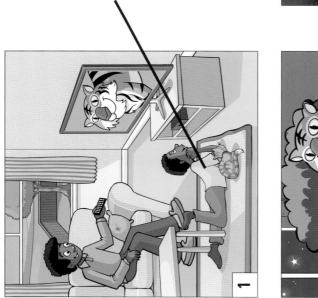

**Odd-one-out**

Blank Page

**Find the Differences**

## Picture Story

Who washed the car?

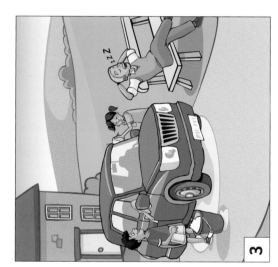

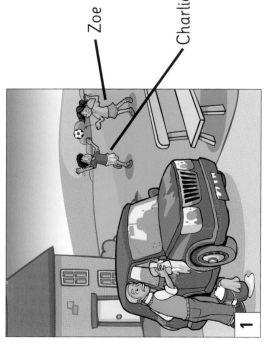

**Odd-one-out**